NIMA

THE COLOR OF
MY SKIN

This Black Woman's Poetry

NIMA

NIMA

THE COLOR OF MY SKIN

Printed in the United States of America

ISBN-13:978-0692678091
ISBN-10:0692678093

Printed by Createspace 2016
Published by BlaqRayn Publishing Plus 2016

NIMA

Table of Contents

NIMA

NIMA

NIMA

86.Mental Note
87.Blue was the New Black
88.Race war
89.Sister Get Down
90.That Funk
91.Bad Bitch
92.Queens Stand UP
93.Stop calling me a Bitch
94.The Sounds of Urban
95.The Sounds of Suburban
96.Big Signs & Bright Lights
97.Mother Earth is crying
98.Color Me Beautiful
99.Love
100.Just because you think I'm sweet

NIMA

Acknowledgments

Thank you for sharing this journey with me. Life is funny. You never know what's in store; people we meet, lives we touch, stories we tell

As always Aaron, Robin, Demetrius, Eliyaas, Lexis, and Jawhara...Thank you for listening to me and my sometimes crazy ideas. Thank you for the moments alone at the table and working around me as I got lost in my writings...

For anyone that paid for a book, CD, or painting..Thank you.

To those that talked behind my back and counted me out as a writer and poet. I will continue on this journey until I get it correct...People like you make a difference in my life more than you know...lol.

NIMA

This body of work has been inspired by some of the events and issues of today. These views are mine and mine alone. With that being said. I love the human race and pray that we can come together as one.

Love and Lips

NIMA

Disclaimer

This body of work has been inspired by some of today's events within my community and culture. I do not speak for anyone but myself. I am not now nor have I ever had the want or need to hate an individual because of the color of their skin. My family and friends represent a beautiful rainbow of people, religions, and culturally diverse backgrounds...

Having said that...

What do I want?
Change!
When do I want it?
Now!
How do I want it?
For everyone in a positive fashion... for all people... especially mine

Love & Lips..

Nima

NIMA

THE COLOR OF
MY SKIN

This Black Woman's Poetry

NIMA

NIMA

Dear Mom

There is nothing that I can say to show you
how much I appreciate all of the things that
you have done for me. You alone have made
many sacrifices. I am sure that mistakes
were made and you were unsure of what to
do but you did the best that you could. How
easy motherhood would be if it came with a
manual and pictures to go along with it. You
started out so young and with so many
responsibilities how could you even have
time to breathe?

Many people can sit on the sidelines and
talk about what they think they know...
What I say to that is... Where were you
when my mother made big Sunday meals
on a hotplate?
Where were you when my mother worked
two jobs and went back to school to further
her education?
Where were you when my mother worked
and sold clothing from the front porch?
When she went to a farm to pick berries
that stained her skin or slept in a cold room
so we could have heat?
Where were you when she walked up to
drug dealers in the street yelling and
threatening them to stay away from her
children?

NIMA

Where were you when she suffered from beatings that my father gave her? Where were you when she had to take five sick children to the doctors and she barely made it herself?

You could have easily given up and yet you pushed harder. You gave more. You put your wants and needs aside and did what you had to do. I'm certain that you spent endless nights crying silently for help with no one to answer. Help did come from time to time and for that I am thankful..

I am saying that I love you and if I ever forget to show you my appreciation, please know that everything I am or will be as a good person is due to The Most High making you my mother.

I love you mommy

Nima

NIMA

Do I Matter?

When I walk down the street and bodies line
the street...I see my skin
When babies cry in arms of grandparents
because daddy sent mommy to the
hospital and he is now being taken away in a
patrol car. I see my skin
When peaceful protest are extinguished by
water hose and police dogs
When pepper spray meets gentle beautiful
black and brown skin
When men are being shot multiple times or
choked to death on city streets
and they can't breathe
When they are placed in patrol trucks
already dead
When black and brown women mysteriously
die in jail cells...I see my skin
Because no matter how wealthy you are or
what title you hold. You are just
a nigger in their eyes!
When I see thousands of men being sent to
prison simply because they don't
have money for lawyers for something as
simple as a traffic ticket or Jay
walking...I see my skin
Don't talk about slavery but let's not forget
9-11
Don't talk about being sold, separated, and
cheated

NIMA

Forget about those dumped in shallow
graves, burned alive, .raped, tortured
and put on display!
All while crying children reached out their
arms to get comfort from the only
love that they know
While fathers and brothers are being
whipped and skinned bodies bloody
and bruised
Having their penis's cut off as to not make
any strong black babies that may
rise up and fight against this oppression!
Spat upon and made to lick the heels of the
tormentor
When you have done any and everything to
try to conquer and kill!

All lives Matter. Yes!!
But before I clean someone else's yard I
have to clean my own first

Because all lives Matter didn't matter until
Black Lives mattered first

Somewhat like the book of Genesis but
some of you will get lost at the tower of
Babel. I'm sure of it

NIMA

I have a Poem in My Heart

Just at the edge of being said
It's strong and powerful
It stands on its own
It will ask for no help
It will make some smile and laughter
will be their support
It will fuel anger and jealousy!
I have a poem in my heart
More like a song that can't go wrong
Inspirational an layered in
expressions
It is conditional; and uncomfortable
It is uplifting and up-building
It sticks to the back of our throat and
you choke on it your entire
life
Strong and weak
Refuses to speak
Beats some down and slaps them
around but only metaphorically
speaking
Like on that good good shit you will
be tweaking
You will beg for it
Look between some legs for it

NIMA

It will stare you in the face
Sit on the tip of your tongue but you
won't recognize the taste
Persistent and cowardly
From birth til death and everything in
between
I have a poem in my heart and it
is...love

NIMA

Black Love

Black Man
Love so on fire
So uncontrolled
So full of color
3 dimensional
Intoxicating and rich
Deep rooted
Kisses like the sun sets my soul on fire
Spinning in slow motion not willing to stop
I need you to build with me
A strong foundation will support and protect
Afro with black fist pick
Sitting on stoops braiding thick hair
Sitting in grandma's rocking chair
Strolling down the summer street
Giving five on the black hand side
Slow drags with red lights and love music
playing in the background
Get down with the get down

NIMA

Sisters of Elements

Hold my hand my sister
I will show you the way
Hold my hand sister and we will find
it together
Our struggle holds us together
Our triumph will lift us
Our troubles will be an example
Our success will show them exactly
what we are made of
Determined and resourceful
Strong and mighty
Life giver
Mother earth
Sister wind
Daughter moon
We came into and gave birth to
ourselves and there is none like us
anywhere

NIMA

Lead

Lead your people!
Stand up and be recognized!
Stand up and be a voice!
Be silent no longer
Take your education and put it to good use
Fight for the rights of those voices that have
been silenced
They need your help
Investigate the lies and untruths
Uncover the history of hate!
Find hidden agendas
Share information and history so that we
are not doomed to repeat it
Stop burning down stores that we need to
buy food and supplies from
There are other ways to protect yourself
besides picking up a gun
Demonstrate leadership
Demonstrate integrity
Learn and share not just your civil rights but
your human rights as well
You are human first and last

You are Rosa Parks
You are Harriet Tubman
You are Sandra Bland
You are Malcolm X
You are Trayvon Martin
You are Michael Brown

NIMA

You are Barack Obama
You are Dr. Martin Luther King Jr.
You are Black Lives Matter
You are Dynasties
You are Kingdoms
LEAD

Written by...Demetrius L. Harris

NIMA

Awakening

Smile in your face
Don't you dare forget your place
Caught up in all this equal opportunity
This we equal stuff
Just a figment of your imagination
Don't let that distract you from the big picture
Too many dogs wagging tails
Telling tales
Aesop's fables
Record labels
Don't believe the hype
Addicted to Skype
Stay glued to the tube
Idiot box
Slick as a fox
So some think
But something strange is happening
Sleeping eyes awakening
Paying attention
Relaxed no more
Watching the front door
Right reasoning taking place
Leaving the ignorance behind
No trace
Now...let us begin

NIMA

Will you Fight for Me?

Will you fight for me when my hands are
bloody from pounding the wall?
Will you speak for me when screaming for
justice has hushed my sound?
Will you stand beside me and lift my fist in
the air when it is all the protest I
have left?
While my brothers and sisters are being sold
as cattle in our prison systems
Unconcerned turn their backs as if they are
not human
Only concerned with their fortune 500's
This king Midas syndrome will shatter their
teeth on the reality of their
world
When   black   lives   matter   is   being
overshadowed by the decision to change
ones sexual identity
They have permanently silenced the voices
of many
My eyes see the hurt and pain in their faces
I   hear   the   cries   from   their
spirits.....FREEDOM TIL I DIE!

Written by..Lexis Harris

NIMA

The Whites Of My Eyes

Face pale as if he had seen a ghost
Fear of the strength of a few
A few that gathered for Bible study in
GODS house
Elderly members and your prayer warriors
Warriors that would have gladly prayed for
him had he only asked
Fear of the power in numbers

They will inherit the earth
They are a mighty people if only they knew
Can't let them find out who they really are

Maybe I can say I feared for my life like
some of my friends in blue
I see her in the corner I will shoot her first
and I will not stop until I am satisfied
I will be labeled a hero to some for this
cowardly deed
My hands are steady and I know what I want
to do and have for some time now
I will not shoot until they see the whites of
my eyes

NIMA

My People

Kissed by the sun
Blessed by The Most High
My hands held high as I sing Praises
Brown like the sweetest sugar
Like caramel or chocolate cookies
Coffee or cocoa
Fine like a perfect wine
My skin drinks in the sun and shines its
brilliance
Black diamond
Minerals
Life giver
Covering the walls of caves and written in
the stars
Continuously rising up from the ashes
Refusing to be pushed aside or left behind
Triumph after triumph
Masters
Attempts have been made to lie and or erase
all contributions and discoveries of my
people and yet the history books and science
continue to prove a point
In the end....

WHAT IS THE POINT?

NIMA

My Brown Skin

My brown skin I love
I like
Never wished to be anything but what GOD
made me
Perfect in his eyes
He makes no mistakes
He needs no double takes
An artist with the perfect brush
Perfect canvas
Perfect subject
My skin glistening in the moon light
Kissed lightly by the sun
I fight for the right to be treated equally but
why should I have to?
I fight for civil rights but why must I?
Imagine if I fought for human rights how
different a world this would be
Me and my brown skin meant to be
Like honey for tea
Like birds in early morning sing
Like church bells ring
If you ain't seen skin like mine
You ain't seen a thing
Sweet and juicy like honey dew
Protecting me from harmful energy
Satisfying and delightful
Picked perfectly with divine hands
Walked this place bare foot and naked in all
of my Queendom

NIMA

Ruling my kingdom
Eyes fixed on the heavens searching for
myself
Found myself in the Garden of Eden
Talking among the trees and wind
Waiting for the world to begin

NIMA

LIVES MATTER!

Black lives Matter!

Human Lives Matter!

Native Live Matter!

Women's Lives Matter!

Children Lives Matter!

Elderly Lives Matter!

Animal Lives Matter!

White Lives Matter!

Cops Lives Matter!

Lives Matter!

What Matters To You?

NIMA

Remember

I remember a time when the
revolution would not be televised!
I remember a time when the
revolution would not be televised!
Open those pretty Brown Eyes!
Open those pretty Brown Eyes!

Because now it comes to you in 3-D with
high definition simultaneously
Broadcast through your media feed at rapid
speed
And you still believe what you see isn't
what you see!
Dogs are still dogs and now they got stun
guns
On your mark
Get set
RUN NIGGA RUN!
Open those pretty brown eyes!
Open those pretty brown eyes!
Master on the plantation
Blue green eyes attempt to run this nation
Planting continued seeds of hater-ation to
our young generations
And they take the bait self-hate
Afraid of their own beautiful black skin
Let's begin again
Afraid of their own beautiful black skin
Passed down from their kin

NIMA

From great great-grandpop making tubs of
gin
When white men slithered with wide eyed
gins
Plotting and; planning on granny's skirt
Snatched her out her sleep and pushed her
down in the dirt
Beat the males of the house into submission
Yet you fools still won't listen
Open those pretty brown eyes!
Open those pretty brown eyes!
Open those pretty fuckin eyes. So you can
see

NIMA

BOYS IN BLUE

Boys in blue
Little boy's blues
Stop doing what you do
Even while the world is watching you could
care less
Some of you are such a mess
You so suppressed
You hate your life and your wife
You would love to take her life
So you hit the streets in order to hit some
peeps
We that pay your salary
Maybe you should retire?
Sign says ..New Gun For Hire
Take your badge and your gun
Just killed all of your fun
Give me those flashlights and handcuffs
Take them home for when daddy likes it
rough

NIMA

Down By the Creek

Down near the creek where my pappy once
was pushed in
He couldn't swim
However, he could hold his breath longer
than anyone I knew
Down near the creek where we met after
church
Where my grandmother was dipped in after
she found Jesus
Down where white women skinny dipped
and blame black boys for looking
Down near the creek where they hung those
same black boys
My momma told me never go down near
the creek but I don't listen and go anyway
Down by the creek where my body was
washed away

Deception

Mass deception for their protection
Continuously injecting
Obligating yourself to his and not our creation
Their devastation
Fill with frustration and aggravation
Yet you refuse to uplift your own nation
Crazy is as crazy does
Follow them as you always do
You fuckin fool
Learned nothing in school
Pay attention to your surroundings
They are drowning and scared shitless
Attempting to take us with them
Keep digging your own ditch for them to throw you in
Self-hate such a sin
Not foundation
Self-hatred
Think self-preservation
Wake up and buy a clue!

NIMA

Stop Right There!

Take your boot out of my brother's
neck!
Keep your riot gear if you please?
Before you shoot to kill at least give us
a chance to stop and
freeze?
Stop killing us as quickly as you can
blink an eye!
I assume you haven't read the poem
Because with all that you do..STILL I
RISE!
Your fear is easy to see
Fear of someone that looks like me
Put down your guns
Pull back your dogs
Turn off your hose
If you try to do right.. then maybe
there would be no fight
In the end when bodies are covering
the streets
When we leave footprints of blood
from the bottoms of our feet

Does it really matter who was right or
wrong?

NIMA

No More Games

I run through the fields of grass..such
luscious green
Falling and chasing clouds
We two laughing and imagining clouds that
make funny faces
Chewing straw before momma rings that
cow bell for supper
Chasing by the creek
Lazy summer days
We throw rocks across the water and pick
berries off of bushes
Suddenly that strange smell
I smelled it before. That smell is so strong
that it stays in your
nostrils for a long time
It sticks to overalls and dresses
More curious we walk towards it
Covering our mouths but eyes wide open
Don't dare breathe in
Eyes water and fear holds us captive
His eyes completely out of his sockets
No shoes
Singing dead mans blues
Pants around his knees
Swinging from the tree

NIMA

Because he smiled at a white woman
Someone hung that beautiful black boy
We played all last week
Down by that creek
Now we don't play down there anymore and
that beautiful black
boy swings all alone

NIMA

1960

Little Girl in the Window

Why won't you come out to play?
Half the day is gone away
All day you sit and watch people go by
Even putting up your hand from time to
time to wave..Hi
You seem so sad up there all alone
As if someone left you there all alone
I wonder if you have dolls to play with.
Little imaginary friends?
That's a big house is it filled with toys?
Do you have parties with lots of noise?
Little girl where is your family?
Do they know that you are there?
Are you feeling sad?
Does anyone care?
I have lots of games for us to play
Lots of toys and even a pet
But we have to wait to play...
Because I haven't been born yet.

NIMA

Coward

Terror in their eyes so they take to guns
We multiply by the millions so they want to
have us on the run
Target practice just for fun
Tried almost everything in the past to rid
this earth of us
Continue to do what you feel you must
We are fine with just us
Make no mistake my love for human kind
surpasses my need to
hate
Hate is such a strong word with powerful
intentions and this is not
who nor what I am
Yet you continue to push and drive home
your selfish and distorted
ways of thinking
You who feed off of negative energy and
allow it to consume you
I will not allow it to do the same to me
I will continue to lift myself up and place
myself above all who
hate
You who kill for pure evil and malice
I am above you and always will be

NIMA

Late Night

It's getting late..I need that fix
Soft kisses to my lips
Heat seeker
Deep breather
Body pleaser
Emotionally satisfied
Won't deny
Let it ride
So many levels to us
Some I can't discuss
But know this much
You consume me
When you love me
I can't see anyone or anything but you
On top or under covers
The perfect lover
Came across one another
It started with my question
You had multiple answers
Hit me up
Break me off
Don't want it soft
Deep. Just perfect for my frame
Play no games
Make me call your name

NIMA

Conversations. Stimulation on some Jill
Scott tip
You make me want to take long walks for
no reason but to look
into your eyes
Child's play is what I call the rest of it
You and I are on some grown loving shit

NIMA

Power for Who??

Power to me and you
Do what we do
By window with curtain pulled slightly back
Because we are black
Where is the voice of Mr. Brown?
Say it loud..(I'm Black and I'm Proud)
Pick yourself up from the ground
Ssh don't make a sound
Listen to our ancestors screaming Rise up
and Take Your Place!
Wipe fear from your face!
Selling dope and shooting your own people
is such a disgrace
Stop saying you feeding your seeds!
You been on that corner for days and your
seeds still eating just beans
You are working for them
But you claim you ain't no slave
You a slave to your grave!
Selling and spreading hate makes you a
traitor!
You are a nigger to the highest power and I
am not talking slang so don't get
it twisted
Pushing your shit straight to the vein of your
brother man
Got them all hooked on dope
Straight to the heart of your community
Wake up

NIMA

Stand up
Take back your power
Rise
You are killing yourself for the love of the
green
You are killing generations so obviously
you working for the other team

NIMA

Hands up!

My blackness is what you fear
When I march and sing you don't hear
When I need your attention and burn things down
Now its hands in the air face on the ground!
Then you remembered who started it
All you are concerned with is who will finish it
In my misunderstanding of myself I forgot who I was and what I
am
I took what you did and took it up a notch or two because that's what
my people do
Now you are on your news portraying me as an animal
I learned by watching you do what you do
If I walk into a store I hear Hands Up!
If I am walking with a group of my peers. Hands Up!
When I choose to protect myself ..Hands Up!
When I protest peacefully.. Hands Up!

NIMA

What will you say when I am all that
stands between you and your
survival?
Will it be Hands Up?

NIMA

Soul Sister

Brown skin
Caramel
Chocolate
Honey dipped
Cool as a fan
Gentle hands
Young miss
Strong willed
God kissed
Sexy and sassy
Sophisticated and classy
Educated and feared
Unafraid to shed tears
Tears don't make you weak
They are the days end washing down
your cheek
Partner and provider
Stand with or get behind her
Invisible crown
Feet never touch the ground
Yet they continue to attempt to bring
you down

NIMA

1950

Shut those windows
Pretend not to see
Shut your mouth
Don't dare ask questions
Be a good little nigger
Walk on the other side of the street
Look at the ground when your eyes
meet
Don't drink out of their fountains
You may be arrested
Stay out of their schools
Baby coons
Got something for you educated folks
Sheets and hoods
Rope for those throats

NIMA

Stand

Wake up sleeping eyes no more
looking the other way
No more pretending not to see
Let us stand strong with one another
Let us look into one another's eyes and
see the good in each man
Though pain and sorrow may live and
breathe there try and break
through
Pass the oppression along no more
Kill the hate
Turn your back on inequality and shout
no more!
Oppression has been chained to us and
implanted in our beings
Break free!
We have the power!
We have the ability!
Do not shout from darkened corners
Do not be a slave to injustices and
inequality
Be a slave to your rights
Your human rights
STAND!

Alabama

Long drive
Dirt road
The sound of chains
Boots march in mud
No street lights
Whispers
Whistles
Children smiling and pointing
Their mothers tell them to look and see
Nigger swing
Angry faces
The sound of many
Reflections of moonlight against tin
stars across fat bellies and
proud chest
No one to care about our screams
Just another nigger hanging in the
south
They killed Dr. King
Why should they care about little old
me?

NIMA

You Are Worth It

This world seems to beat you down and
your troubles may be many
Know my love that you are worth time
The time it takes to get to know you and
appreciate you and form a bond
before they are asking to love your body
Know that you are worth an explanation
when something isn't the way it
should be and you don't understand why
Know that you are worth taking home to
meet his or her parents
You are worth that High school Diploma
That College Degree
You are worth that Job that makes you
happy
You are worth it
When having your dreams come true seems
like a place in Never Never land
It may be a battle
It may be hard
It may cause you to sacrifice some things
In the end you make the choice to stay
strong
To keep in prayer
To fight the good fight
To hold your head up
My Sister!
My Sistah!
You Are Worth It!

NIMA

The Good Fight

Fighting to be fighting
Fighting for the right to live in peace
Fighting for the rights of any human
being
Fighting because we like to fight
Fighting to make a statement
To make an example
To start trouble
Fighting because it is all we learned how
to do
Fight for who?
Fight for you!
Fight for us!

Fight against injustice!

NIMA

I AM BLACK

Dark as night
Black as coal
Soil from where I gave birth to myself
Holding the stars
Vast and unexplained
Unexplored and unmolested
Intriguing and mysterious
Strong like coffee
Feared and wanted
Hunted and haunted
Complicated and though they try...
Never duplicated

NIMA

Hands in the Air

My hands in the air screaming for justice
My voice yells stop killing my people
My heart breaks for the lives that have been
taken out of sheer hatred
My feet march because marching seems to
get attention
My eyes hold back tears because I will not
give you the pleasure of seeing
me break
You wont give justice
Now I must take
Can't promise it will be pretty
May even burn half a city..

Let's pray not

NIMA

New World

Mathematics I have shown thee
How to survive in this new world you have
come to know
Dynasties where I once ruled
Robbed and raped of land and commodities
for selfish use
Stripped of natural resources and left for
dead
I am still here!

You have crossed land and sometimes
oceans to gaze upon my beauty and then
destroy it!

Bringing disease and pestilence
Confusion is your trademark
Kidnapping my brothers and sisters for
personal gain
Some have same skin as mine others do not

Sit at my table and break bread with me only
to take it without permission
I would have given unto you if only you
would have asked
Travel over oceans
Losing many along the way
Stuffed and packed in lower levels
The ocean has cried many times since the
voyages

NIMA

It is angry and swallows up and brings
forth destruction of its own now New
lands, new enemies, new way of life

This new world where people of my skin
have been since the beginning of time yet
we do not speak the same language

I no longer walk in silk and satin
No more turquoise and ivory

It has been stripped away and sold off to
the highest bidder along with my pride

It has been beaten out of me after they sold
my parents and children into this thing
called slavery

I am now a shell of who and what I used to
be and they are now happy

NIMA

Wind Between My Fingers

Wind between my fingers as we move
into the future..
I, as a little child exploring and
laughing as it moves through me..
I felt GOD move through me!
I noticed in small creatures prior to
this day but today was something
different
It tickled the tips and caressed my
palms and I knew it was the...

CREATOR

Win At Life

Today is the start of forever
Racing the sun
Hiding from the moon
Counting stars
Naming trees
Watching oceans play host to
creatures never seen by human eyes
Voyages unsure of
Stay forever living until tomorrow is
no more

NIMA

Double Up

Kiss then kiss me harder
Love then love me harder
Make love then make love to me more
intensely
Live then live louder
Pray then pray stronger
Life...live it to the fullest

Peace

A little piece for me
Time alone to think
A moment to enjoy
Free from
Questions that need answering
Looks that need to be explained
Emotionally drained
A quality for me to be me
Just to be free
To daydream uninterrupted
To think of lands beyond
Before returning to this one
Just a little peace without resting in it

NIMA

Without

One day without your voice
Your touch
Your laughter
Your sarcasm

Now enters sadness Uncertain
emotions Unwanted thoughts
Incredible distractions Uncertain
reactions

Guilty

Pulled over for no reason
Only car in their sight

Live or die depends on the mood
Identified as being black

Covered in flashing red and blue lights
Every moment more intense

Be very still and very quiet
Right to remain silent unless they ask a
question
Utter the wrong word and it could be
your last

Take nothing for granted
All guns pointed at you

Lives Matter at this very moment
It seems like a bad dream

but you better not blink
Talk slow

NIMA

You are guilty of driving while black

Written By
Robin O. Langley

NIMA

How Should I Feel?

They are killing my people in the
streets!
Without warning just aim and shoot as
you please
Stop dead in your tracks
Shot in your backs
Held in police cells
Dead before you can make bail
One phone call home
May be your last before one to the
dome
Like picking flowers from a field
Killed because you took too long to
yield
Don't make it a black and white thing?
I would rather not
A few of others but mainly my skin
tone are the ones being shot
You will not be judged by the content
of your character but by the
color of your skin..
As if my skin is a sin
Protest signs go up
Hands go up
Black bodies go down

NIMA

Pulled over by the boys in blue
Don't make a sound
You know your rights and they don't
care
Bullets flying everywhere
Taking the lives of young and old
Sounds like stories from down south
that grandpop told
We are within a war zone watching it
all unfold
I was raised that we are all created
equal and should have the same
chance
But those red and blue lights sing a
war dance

Stop the Violence

NIMA

Once

Once was
No more
Life travels
Darkened roads
Search out
Fire behind eyes growing

Text Faces

Smiling from ear to ear
Bewilderment and wonder
Angry face move fingers quickly to
respond
Confused and hesitant with crunched
eyebrows
Blushing cheeks are followed by
biting bottom lips
Frustration sighs consume some
morning rush hours
Others nod in disapproval and delete
all becomes the only option

NIMA

Morning Glow

Morning glow suits you
Is it because of me?
Is it because of us?
Send you into the world with me
covering you
After shocks tremble your world
through-out your day
Taking a moment to reflect and a secret
smile across your face
Just traces of us

Moments

Intimate moments
Candles
Darkness
Slow jams in my ear
Bed and pillows fluffed
Favorite blanket
Fresh from the shower
Tee shirt
Something sweet and sexy to sip
My pen and pad
My creativity on pages
Pages where everything is limitless
and maybe over the top
Maybe too much for some
For some not enough
For me...just right
Sometimes the perfect night
Love these moments

Willing

Willing to be imprisoned by all of him
Captured from the start and
bound by emotions Pulled in
by attraction and spirituality
Our like minds inhale and
exhale and exhale us I taste
him on my tongue and in my
nostrils Strange at first and
afraid
Sharing smiles and stories
Enchanted and exquisite was this

Long awaited
The kiss on the collarbone opened the
door
The tight embrace threw open the
windows
The whispers in the ear laid me down
The walk through my temple wrapped
chains around us
Meticulously examined and discovered
by love
So tell me...when did you fall in love
with poetry?

NIMA

So tell me...when did you fall in love
with me?

NIMA

Love Like This

To live and love
Love as hard as possible
Love until it fills your heart with
excitement
Love so hard it scares you
Love when all else says don't
Love like water running over rocks
Clear, transparent, continuously
forever flowing
From beginning to beginning
because there is no end
Just lakes, rivers, ponds, oceans, and
falls
Like breeze through trees
Love like soft snow falling from a
night sky

NIMA

Rain Drops

For every thorn there grows a beautiful
rose
Every cloudy sky brings rain drops
with smiling faces to clean
mother earth once again
For the splashing of mud filled puddles
for little boots
Boots that make tracks across our
hearts as we grow older and
learn to appreciate them more

NIMA

Let's Make a Funny Romantic Movie

You will see me walking down the street
In between everyone we meet
We will smile and gaze for a while
Noise will break our stare and thoughts will
take us there
You will be reading Aesop's Fables
disguised by a book cover brandishing two
turn
tables
And I shall be reading something by...Me
You will ask if you can carry my book just
so that you can open it and take a closer
look
Nodding your head to a perfect beat that I
don't hear. You make it very clear...
That I am interesting
He quotes Malcolm
I quote Martin
My skin is his skin
Understanding the same struggles
He loves natural but understands my perm
Maybe one day meet for a cup of tea
You know just you and me?
And let the rest of the world just be
I will smile and you will wink
We will share a laugh
I stop to think
Then say ok
Let's link up one day
Walking away smiles are my umbrella yet I
have always hated that saying
Til we meet again
My shy grin
We liked old-school

NIMA

Him-Hip-Hop
Me-Doo Wop

Halfway up the street
Jogging feet
Turning to see you with my book in hand
Hmm I think I like this man
Should it ever become clear to me?

No numbers exchanged
I guess it wasn't meant to be

NIMA

When the Time Comes

When I go please remember me??
Think about the laughter that we shared
Dancing for no reason specifically
Breaking out into song just because
Snapping photos to capture life's precious
moments
Catch me watching the sky as I often did
and playing connect the dots with
clouds
Writing because I loved it so
Making people happy
Talk about me in loud voices and in
whispers
Maybe I touched a life in a special way.
At least I hope I did?
Not always in agreement with any and all
but open to suggestions
Forgive me if I hurt or offended you in
anyway? That was not my intention.
I have asked The Most High for
forgiveness and hope that you can find it in
your heart should you find yourself on the
list. Praying that my short
comings never have to be suffered by my
children
Doing my best is all I can humanly do
Write a story, a poem, a song, paint a
picture, laugh until my stomach hurts
Tastes food that feels like an oral orgasm

NIMA

Dance* until my feet hurt
Be loved
Fall in love
Love until it hurts
Pray every day that The Most High
blesses you with things
Hold my grandchildren and their children
See something new and beautiful each day
Hopefully we were friends and if not
hopefully you respected me
I hope some of my writings were
enjoyable to you
That was my point

Love and Lips...

Nima

NIMA

Young Old Lady

The smell of her cooking when you
know that the gas was turned
off
The warmth of your bedroom while
the heat has been shut off
The chill in her bones because she
has taken too many cold baths
so that you could have hot water
The fear in her heart when her baby
doesn't call to check in
The look in her face when she feels
that she has failed you
Emotionally beat down from past
relationships
Torn between obligations and desires
Mentally running away every chance
she gets
Putting her own feelings aside
Temporary fix comes from the
bottom of a can
She still does not understand
Dealing with an on again off again
man
Sometimes it's hard to understand

To

To know beyond this
To feel outside the box
To walk the wind
To play the sun
To inhale the now
To put away the so-so
To capture the what ifs the Never Evers
To stand in the moments
Dreams and fantasies
We all have that wish upon a star moment
and if not..

NIMA

Can't Wait

Pen erect ready for battle
Tip holding back explosions
Attempting to maintain a cool hand
Gazing upon the opponent
Ink slowly begins to drip
I ain't trip
Pull back think cool thoughts

Now slowly start the pace
Slow and steady it's no race

Waited for big words that I couldn't
understand
Waited for consciousness
Waited for intelligent exchange or
intellectual stimulation
Moons and stars
Gathering of galaxies
Explanation of human existence
Gripping my pen nearly choking it
Waited to grab my dictionary
Pen about to bust...and...and...and
Dead air space...damn

Wondering

She wonders where he came from
Stars that twinkle at night
Sun beams that slide through your
curtains
Another realm
Fourth or fifth planet over
Eyes look through and see every layer
of everything
Dance between raindrops because they
can
Love out loud in silence
Skin electrical
Yet walking in with rubber body suit
Kisses like fire
Touches like flames burning souls
Love unexplained

My Dance

The dance of a thick sistah
So seductive though she hardly tries
They sway to their own rhythm
No twerking necessary
Speak and threatens though she means
no harm
Calls for unwanted attention at times
So she slows her pace.
Only   to   take   away   her
stride..no..no..no..!!
Her mother and father gave her those
hips and thighs these breast
Hips that gave shelter to Black Queens
and a King!
Breasts that gave live and nutrition to
Blackness
That helped to slumber those tired and
restless loved ones
I will continue my stride and you will
continue to watch as I walk

NIMA

Much More

Much More Inspired

By Signed and Sealed Refusal to
invade

Over flows Streams Mountains

Blue skies Birds sing softly

Why?

You tell me?

Mother

Pain follows closely
Strangles you nearly dead
Allows you to see clearly
Sometimes what you don't want to see
Met pain the day I came into this world
Came down the canal into a pool of blood
and mucus
With screams of agony
Near death
Breathing shallow
Heart races
Beads of sweat dance from forehead to
upper lip
She is calling GOD
But he hasn't shown up yet
Reaching out now for those familiar hands
that no longer reach for mine
She suffered through that pain long ago
Welcoming me into this world she and pain
are on a first name basis.

NIMA

Simple Things Not So Simple

Grass sings
Blue skies cry out
Butterflies put on a colorful performance
Lovers kiss passionately
Bees make love make honey
Summers gentle breeze flows around us
Makes us funny that way
Some things so predictable and funny
Some things are what they are
Love is love and nothing else can be its
substitute
Fire place dances
Illuminating love
Illuminating nights making for a sexy scene
Childish laughter for no reason
God give me the simple things

NIMA

Unwanted Visitor

Dark gloomy clouds hang low
Eyes that look nowhere in particular
Gazing aimlessly into the atmosphere
Searching for signs of love
Life's meaning
Searching souls for common ground
Shadows at every corner expecting a piece
of your soul
Sometimes having no more to give
Ready to die
Left empty
Wishing pain to go far from you
Death knocks and you fear that it may come
without being asked to come in

NIMA

Dearest Mother

Mother where are you?
I have looked all through the house
and my calls have gone
unanswered
I have shouted and no one has come
running
I fell down outside and bruised my
knee
Who will kiss the pain away?
Who will bake me cookies and tell me
that all will be ok?
Does this mean that I am a man now?
No more hugs and stories
No more saying my prayers with me
at night before I fall to sleep
The boys outside said they don't have
mothers and they don't need
them
Will I be like them?
A real man!
They have guns and stand on corner
Will I be like them?
Momma where are you?
You still don't answer
Where is my father?

NIMA

Does he ask about me?
I'm afraid mother
I want to cry
The men on the corner said (real Men
don't cry)
Is that true momma?
Momma?

NIMA

Playing Big Girl

Until the end of time oozed through black
speakers
Her ears and senses awaken
Every touch like perfect strokes of an artist
brush
Fingers trace her emotions
Whispers make love to ears
Deep breath through clinched teeth before
biting bottom lips were
popular
Young woman in all her adult attitude took
every bit and then
some
Open her mouth in ecstasy to let her low
screams fill his room. But
Prince beat her to sound
Brown bodies sweat to nights they won't
forget

NIMA

All You Do

For all the fights in the middle of the
street
For all the spankings when I skipped
school
For coming home when you didn't
have to afterlife showed you a
prettier picture
For not tossing me out in the trash like
yesterday's news
For trying your best when all others
sat and watched and pointed
fingers
When you warned me ahead of time
what would happen before it
happened
For working two jobs and having a
hustle to put food on the table
For keeping a roof over our heads
Because life was not as kind to you as
it was to some people
Because people continue to point out
your mistakes when they
themselves have made more than a
few

NIMA

When you can point the finger at
many and say "you did this to
me" and yet you say nothing

You continue to laugh

To dance
To love
To smile

Thank You Mommy

Love Is

Will he always love her?
Days of youth long gone
Fine lines are now heavy wrinkles
Legs that once wrapped around his
back now barely make it up the
stairs
Forgetting the names of places they
have been to
12 bottles of pills line the table that he
serves her daily
Sex is no longer an issue but intimacy
is for all of her days
The smell of her cooking has left the
kitchen
Pots no longer rattle
Sometimes conversations are one sided
Perms and weaves have destroyed her
hair texture beyond repair
Will he always love her?
After the rain has fallen and all that is
left are puddles of mud
When rainbows are no longer beautiful
reminders in the sky but a
description of a group of persons

NIMA

True love is like a timeless mirror
It sees what you want it to see

Love is timeless and ageless
And yes he will still love her

NIMA

Loving Utopia

In the middle of the night and just before
morning rise..our spirits meet and
make love.
Goosebumps cover me and a sensational
tingle runs down my spine
I feel him in every way possible
I hear his voice
Now awake his presence I feel
Turning to no one behind me..
Eyes closed
Deep breathing
I find myself opening my mouth just a bit
to catch a sip from his lips

NIMA

Smile for Me

Sad eyes for too long
Little girl grew too soon
Missing laughter as little children do
Swings go but with the innocent
childhood of others
Too often seen shadows in the dark
Never coming to light
Monsters under the bed and in the
closet waiting for the Prince to
rescue her from the dungeon
Tears held back or pushed away afraid
for anyone to see so you cry
yourself to sleep
Cry with your now growing belly
Praying that this life will
unconditionally love you
Rain brings umbrellas of lovers
standing underneath
Yet you sit by your window waiting
for someone yet no one
He made promises
They are too quickly broken
Too many interruptions
Young love has gotten old very fast
She still finds some reason to smile

NIMA

Protect and Serve

Calling all cars!
Prepare for battle is the call!
Shoot until they fall!

All are not out of control
All are not evil
Some continue to wear their badge with
honor and dignity
Some still protect and serve
Cruelty is everywhere
Beautiful lands out of control
Beautiful hands that have saved and pulled
black lives out of pits
Blaring blue and red lights should not mean
death
It should not promote panic or fear

Rushing pregnant black mothers to
hospitals just in time to bring black
babies into this world
Coming to my mother's rescue when his
beatings nearly took her life
Providing blankets and teddy bears to little
scared ones on cold dark nights
while parents yelled at the top of their lungs
Walking tough neighborhoods after dark to
keep some order
For chasing suspects on foot without
pulling out your weapon

NIMA

To those that have to pull your weapon and
will only truly brandish it if and
when all options have failed
For loving your job because you truly want
to make a difference and matter
in a good way
People hate you for the acts of some of your
peers
It's not fair but unfortunately it comes with
the territory
Just ask any BLACK MAN

Written By: Robin Langley

NIMA

In My Father's House

Dear GOD protect me while I hide
I hear his footsteps coming closer
Remember me if I should perish in
your house of worship
What made this walking, talking,
hateful man decide to come to
our home and kill your visitors or did I
just answer my own
question
The little girl lying next to me is
pretending to be dead
I hope he goes the other way
Monsters in our midst
Bullets rip through skin of my kin
Face down in pools of blood
Prayers were all that we came after
Diabolical
Demonic
Filled our house with hatred
While our children are thrown to the
ground with guns in their
backs..
Killers are wearing bullet proof vest
and taken to fast food
restaurant

NIMA

Where was the bullet proof vest for those innocent lives?

NIMA

Old Paint Brushes

Old paint brushes
Stroked canvas too many times to
remember
Dependable always waiting for new
colors
Some have lost their luster and
thickness
Full of mixed colors from previous
paintings
Still attempt to stand tall in the eye of
the artist
Gazing upon it and growing worried if
it is to be capable of
another portrait

Beautiful

Out of his mouth to say how beautiful she
was
Her obligation to family
The way she walked
The way she spoke
Her voice
Those hips
Those lips
That street corner under the light kind of
thing
Now...
Screams and yells
Clinched fists
Angry teeth showing me how hate looks
How insecurities look
Reddish brown imprints cover my arms
In between babies are being conceived
Black blue eyes unlike eye shadow
False love
Lies and deception
Hopes and dreams of one day being loved
Too young to truly understand what love
means yet old enough to
understand that it can't be like this
Drunken rage
Open handed smacks that nearly shatter
teeth
Guns look so appealing to me at this point

NIMA

Battle cries and neighbors now with porch
lights on peek out of their
curtains but wait for blood shed before
helping
He that once was looked upon to be her
savior
Now her nightmare

And it all started with those beautiful
marks on her skin

NIMA

Fools Walk In

Misunderstanding signals Assumptions
far too often
Make understanding so hard Failing to
look deep
Finding the heartbeat
Some easily set on the path to it Others
trip and fall never to find it
Explanations and disconnections

NIMA

Imagine That?

In my mind I have imagined being
white
Being without daily struggles of black
America
Without stereotype
I have thought what if I didn't have to
get stopped by the police as
I drove down the road?
What if I walked with groups of
friends without being watched or
followed?
What if they didn't fear me?
What if I had not surpassed in every
aspect even the negative?
What if?
What if I stopped all of this
foolishness because I love being
Black!

Searching

Searched my brain attempting to find
the reason
Reason we created
God took over and allowed
I am grateful for this
Searching for self-love may lead you on
a different path
Follow that path until self-love has
been found
Not everyone needs a yellow brick
road
Overstood?

NIMA

Children and Fireflies

Minds dance in the wind
Carries laughter
Laughter plays like fire flies
Elude captivity
Water makes rocks smooth as silk
Laughter like young children uncaring
of danger
Let your mind live like children and
fireflies

NIMA

Seen Her Before

She sat on her porch watching the
children run by
Watching the day go away
Sitting and rocking. Drinking her tea
Yelling for babies to "get out of that
street!"
Reminding them boys to get off the
corner
She has no children of her own yet she
has raised many
"Go round to the store and get me a
pack of Virginia slims and tell
the man they for Miss Mary and you
keep the change now hear"
As a young child I thought she was so
strange
Telling my momma when I was about
to fight
Who gave her that right?
She always in somebody business
Told the girl up the street.. "Don't you
carry that baby like that?"
Told her not to pay them doctors no
never mind and babies are

supposed to be fat that means they eating good
She was so strange and always old
Now a days I'm Ms. Mary telling children stay out the street and
stay off those corners
Ms. Mary stayed on that porch just rocking until they took her
away I believed they said she was 92 years young. I miss that old
lady. Sitting in her rocking chair. Smoking her Virginia Slims
Minding everyone's business
We need her now
Now I got me a rocking chair for my porch
But I like Newports

If

Imagine if rappers didn't talk about guns
Imagine if they didn't promote shooting
dudes for fun
Imagine if we didn't see videos with big
asses little skirts
Pretend dead bodies lying face down in the
dirt
Imagine spending our money on black
businesses only
Spending mad loot with the other man and
your shit still phony
Imagine never giving your money to a
company that said they don't like
selling to blacks
Imagine if we could take all of our dollars
right back
What about for every negative rap video
you put a black person through
school
Imagine how powerful a tool
Imagine telling your younger sisters and
brothers not to sell dope
Could be so beautiful yet you knuckleheads
still talking bout...NOPE
Imagine if (DO THE RIGHT THING)
wasn't just a movie with one of the
most memorable lines... RADIO!!
Imagine if the killers in our community
really had to go

NIMA

Imagine if you read your artist contract
Imagine if you had information that was
right and exact
What a wonderful world this would be. If
you would stop killing and let life
be
Too many wars out here to fight
Yet you kill our own people
That ISH ain't right!
Imagine if you stop going to jail in large
numbers
Imagine if you didn't think like the crowd
Imagine if nothing played on the radio but
(JAMES BROWN...I'M BLACK
AND I'M PROUD?)
Imagine playing ball from sun up to sun
down
Imagine that no one came to shoot up the
playground

I F

NIMA

How Far Have We Really Come?

Madness and confusion
Souls penetrated
Lives extinguished
Perish Senseless
Tortured emotions
How long must this go on before we
learn to live together?
Sharing what The Most High has given
all as a gift
Why must we fight for what is
naturally free?
Millions of lives destroyed for oil, land,
natural minerals
Outsiders invade homes to collect
riches that belong to native
communities
Outcry!
Outrage!

NIMA

My Black Jesus

Growing in a household where my natural
father is felt but not seen
My stepfather has cared for me since birth
He loves my mother and me
As I grow I notice that all of my physical
attributes differ from those of my
household
Growing into knowledge of self-caused
conflict among my parents and
siblings
My hair like wool
My skin as if the color of soil
I am watched at every angle
Eyes hate because of who I am or what I
represent
Rolling around with my crew the true
meaning of ride or die
But it's some foul niggas in my circle
plotting on my demise
My main man will do me in
Nail me to the cross and after this fool sat
at my table, ate my food, drank
my wine
He called me his brother
He got with those fools across town and
acted as if he didn't even know me
Betrayal at its best and you wonder why
my eyes stay red like fire.

NIMA

And with all of that. Would I die for my
nigga??
I already did

NIMA

Listen

I listen with my ears at attention
Vibes got me snapping my fingers
Bobbing my head to the words she said
So well put together lyrically balanced with
a pretty ass bow
Nouns and verbs I never heard
Got me saying words like dope and word
Taking me back to a time I use to like
Got me thinking damn that's hype
I'm like in some daze
Like purple haze

Calling one another kings, queens, and
GODS
Sisters and Brothers
Showing love to one another
Thought maybe I drank the cool aid and Jim
Jones was just around the
corner

Grabbing my dictionary looking in my
glossary
Short quick joints
Right to the point joints
Got me on my revolutionary boy
Others got me like all in my girly box
looking for my favorite toy
Roller coaster ride
You can't hide

NIMA

Shit, this be like needle to the vein
Have you calling its name
Keep trying to walk away from it and it be
on some..
Hey you
Come here
Give me a kiss
Right then and there I knew he had me
Damn you poetry
Just will not let me be
I pretend that I need to be free
But you got me

Inspired

Inspired thought
Bring about intelligent conversation
Discussion of racism
Yet we smile and pretend to not see it
Though it races towards us at rapid
speed
360 degrees of it all
Now who you gonna call?
When this begins
I don't want to plant seeds like those of
hatred did
I want to encourage love of u and I
Eyes wide closed
Looks in the opposite direction
You must acquire the thirst
Foundation first
Self-Love

Biblical

From Genesis chapter one to
Revelations when we have seen our
final sun
This has been foretold in description
each level of depiction
On walls encrypted
Purposely strategically placed here
This appointed time
This perfect place
Prescribed space
Layers of regret suddenly dissolved
Love they revolved around positive
energy

NIMA

The Truth Is..

Feeling him from not too far away
His scent
His Power
His whisper
Sexy cloaked in intelligence
Passion dripped in facts
Erotic smoothly layers every inch
Strength handled with care
Feeling him when I sleep
His ocean way too deep
Surrounded by stars that twinkle because he
is
Confident in his stride because he is
Dope lines
Perfect beats
Ready willing and able
Only chick in his stable
Love my juicy lips
Speak to my soul
Speak through me out into the universe

Ladies and gentlemen we interrupt this
program to give you a word from our
sponsors...
I don't want to write!
I don't want to write!
Another fuckin poem or piece

NIMA

I don't want to show myself to undeserving
unappreciative ignorance
To those that really could care nothing about
true me...only about what I can
do for them
Pretending to spread peace and spreading
poison instead
Hanging with the clique
Come on man...you too old for that shit
They say be true to yourself but.. what if
being true to self....Hurts someone
else?
So judgmental wearing fake smiles and fake
congratulatory gestures
Not even waiting until you turn your back
before the knife comes out
An arm here
A leg there
A thigh here
My heart over there

Tossed out like yesterday's garbage
Struggle within myself
Against me
For everyone else
When is my time?
Is my time meant to happen?
Is it off in the fairy tale land that I love so
much?
If I open up a book will it reveal itself to me?

NIMA

If I cried would magic flowers grow from
my tears?
Would anyone care?
Maybe I will put out a piece that starts
with...1 can feel you growing inside
of me pushing... love hard deep within me
Spreading my wings to your delight and
multiple orgasms now take flight
And ending it with a poet's kiss of the lips
that make men man their
battleships
I know!
I will find the longest words in the dictionary
or the most profound phrase in
the American language and make that my
opening line

Close it with quotes by Dr. King, Brother
Malcolm or Dr. Maya Angelou
Because when folks so loosely throw those
names in the air without even the
proper respect the crowd goes wild...
The crowd goes wild!!
The crowd goes wild!!
It's like the best sports commentator of the
most long awaited game of the
season
And for what reason?
Using words like metaphors and meticulous
Ten thousand moons ago
Universe

NIMA

Black love
Verses and flows
Now watch the crowd grow

Maybe if I cut my wrist and opened up the
life flow of me would I then get an ounce
of what I have given you returned to me?

Would you then concern yourself with me or
would I just be... another dead poet?

Now back to your regularly scheduled
programming

Loving you against all odds
 Against negative forces
 Loving you is never hard
 No heels... with painted toenails to match
 fingertips
 Center stage...our perfect performance

 My rose petal map leading to candles that
 light the way to your favorite dish
 My heart racing...attempting not to rush
 Red wine sipped slowly pushing my
 excitement to a new level
 You grip my hips...your face buried
 between tits
 Warm honey drips
 Sexy honey dip

NIMA

Lost in lust
 You lost in lips...both sets
 Me...well beyond wet
 My mind transported and transformed
 Thirsty... I drink your beads of sweat
 Us...looking for the perfect beat
 As we rock Bells

 Teaching me all things black
 Needle to the track
 Records blasting true hip hop
 Never that whack ass rap
 We bang to B.Boy beats
 We sex to true hip hop non stop
 We ride to meticulous metaphors
 From the bed to the floor
 Fuck til neighbors bang on the door

 Then we ride some more

I want to scream!!!!

Scream so loud that it shakes the heavens
and alerts the angels that I need to scream!

They know before the thought even comes

into completion that I am in Need I am

ALIVE!!

NIMA

Does anyone here realize or recognize that?
Walking through this optical illusion of blue
skies and green grass.

Walls closing in... is what I see
Trees blow in the wind and days turn to
years yet... what have I done?
Nothing!

Nothing on a scale of nothing to be weighed
against nothing
Forces pulling at my flesh
Ripping at my emotions
Darkness is the perfect cover-up
The perfect blend to shield my face from the
truth behind it all
What exactly is the truth?

Is my darkness confusion because I am
uncertain about the truth
Is the darkness my friend?
My lover?
My hope?
My dope?

It sits and waits for me even in daylight
It goes nowhere
Blanketing me when all I want to do is run!
Run away barefoot and naked to a land far
from here

NIMA

To the end of nowhere yet to the beginning
of everything

NIMA

Help!

The smile is a cover up
I am screaming inside and no one
hears me!
The tears are invisible flowing down
My cries are not being heard !
Slowly I sit in the corner waiting to live
and yet dying
Help me stand. I promise to walk on
my own!
Help me to the table and I will feed
myself
Walk by me no more

NIMA

No Means No!

Late date
Smiles
Great conversation
Two adults
Mood mellow
Introductions made some time ago
Taking it slow
Attraction There

Kiss goodnight taste like another
Wait ok...a little too much tongue
Now I'm done
Aggression shows...now he has to go
Wait get off of me!
This wasn't meant to be
Reaching under my skirt
Pulling on my shirt
Scratches to his face!
Now he has a taste
Reality sets in
He knows its time to go
No Means No!

NIMA

Mental Note

I do make a difference and I am
important and yes...

I DO MATTER!

And don't you forget it!

NIMA

Blue Was the New Black

My beautiful black skin changed
overnight so it seems
Ripped from my body
Pieces of me left on the sink
On the floor
For so long I ran away in my
imagination until I found my courage
Found my footsteps
My skin now Blue from constant one
sided battles
To this day I refuse to wear blue
Blue was the new Black...
But not anymore.!

NIMA

Race War!

My People First!

No, My People First!

We Matter!

No, We Matter!

NIMA

Sister Get Down

She way back to the 60's
Fist in the sky
Real high
Mink coat to the floor
Gun in hand standing by the door
Ready for war
Brown fist
Tight fist
Praying it won't take that
Preparing to die just because she's
Black
Protest for freedom gone way too far
Jumped in the getaway car
Fighting the man
Took a stand
She ready to go round for round
Sister Get down

NIMA

That Funk

That drum beat
That guitar skeet Drips with
vibrations Super sexy sensation Toe
tapping
Booty slappin
Hand clappin Shoulders bounce

Bad Bitch

I don't need a man
I got my own money
I don't need a man for shit
I'm a Bad bitch
My hair stay tossed
My shoes cost a grip
Like I said...I'm the shit
My car stay gloss
I'm a boss
My heart is cold
Your conversation is real old
I'm a bad bitch
I'm lonely
I'm sad
Fake smiles are my business
No one to share anything with
Cold bed
Microwave dinners
Take out for one
Isolation has begun
I'm a bad bitch

NIMA

Queens Stand Up!

Queens Stand Up!

Queens stand Up!

Kings take your place

NIMA

The Sound of Urban

Bottles break
Ghetto snakes
Babies cry
Young die
Lights camera action
Quick fast satisfaction
Dope boys on every block
Hoes mark the spot
No Justice No peace
Black Lives Matter

NIMA

The Sounds Of Suburban

Grass being cut
Paper boy on time
Ice cream truck rides by
Apple Pie in the window
Bodies buried in the basement down
below

NIMA

Big Signs & Bright Lights

Shiny things attract children
They like to dream
Pretty things go by
Hands outreached to the sky
Need to catch those pretty things
That girl wants a diamond ring
That one never wants to grow old
Though impossible
Everything else could be yours for just
a portion of your soul

#Let's make A Deal

Mother Earth Is Crying
So we must be dying
Wipe her tears

NIMA

Color Me Beautiful

Brown, Black, Tan, Caramel, Chocolate
Flawless
Ebony
Brown sugar
Black as Night
Black as Coal
Oak

Full Brown lips..
Pink Lips

Love

Strong
Pure
Before the dictionary had a meaning
for it
Before time on earth
Before anyone sang a song or wrote
about it
Fire
Sexy
Intimate
Exciting
Its yearning
Uplifting
Creating
It's Me
It's You

NIMA

Just Because You Think I'm Sweet

Just because you think I'm sweet
Because when I take off my shoes I got
pretty feet
Let me hit you off with a lil heat

Peel that cap as a matter of fact
Don't give a fuck if we go way back
Get the shit right as a matter of fact

My tattoo says spit shit
cause I got lock on your tip bitch
don't think Imma ever miss shit
cause you a corny nigga tryna flip shit

You were alright for a minute though
Til you popped fly on sistah yo
Now I'm comin for your ass real slow
Dots lined up on your whole crew bro
So you see the hit in 3d yo
Don't like the way that my pistol blow
Guess that's the way that some shit go

NIMA

Nima Shiningstar-El resides in Philadelphia, the city of brotherly love with her family and is the author of "Poem, Quotes and Thoughts Provoked", "Nima's Nights", and this her third release "The Color of My Skin".